The b
with the
apples on
his tusks

Life in the Newport Wetlands 7500 years ago

By

Jennifer Foster

Everything in this book is based on our archaeological digs at Goldcliff, South Wales. Go to the back of the book to find out more.

Supported by The National Lottery Heritage Fund

Printed by Living Levels Landscape Partnership 2019

www.livinglevels.org.uk

ISBN 978-1-912804-75-7

To Martin who excavated the site, and Ellies and
Sarah who played in the mud every summer

The Boar with the Apples on his Tusks

Once upon a time, 7500 years ago to be precise, a family lived in a hut on the edge of the Severn in Wales. This is the story of that family.

The family is Mam, Dad and their children: son Wolf, daughter May Bud and baby daughter Crane. Their dogs are called Wuff and Sandy. They live with Mam's parents, Mamgu and Dadcu*. Mam's two sisters, Aspen and Rainbow, also live with them. Rainbow and her partner Wild Wave have two children, Petal and baby Rose.

*Mamgu and Dadcu mean Nanny and Grandad in Welsh. You pronounce them Mamgee and Dadkee.

CHAPTER 1

From Summer Meet to Summer Camp

If you stood on Goldcliff Island looking down the Severn Estuary towards the sea, on a warm summer afternoon 7500 years ago, you might have seen something moving on the river, close to the northern bank. It would be so far away you wouldn't realise what it was and then gradually it would come into focus, six small wooden boats loaded with things and people. They were coming with the incoming tide, which made it easier to paddle upstream.

The group was on the last step of their journey from The Meet to Summer Camp. They did this every year so they knew where they were going. They were home for the summer to catch fish. Finally they reached Goldcliff, so called because the sun shining on the cliff made it shine like gold. The boats struggled up the river and turned in behind the island. They had arrived! The grown-ups jumped overboard into the shallow water and pulled the boats up on the shore. May Bud and her sister Crane had travelled in Mam's boat. They leapt out and, with their brother Wolf and cousin Petal, ran into the camp. There were the skeletons of the summer huts with the remains of last year's reed thatch, but nothing else to show that anyone had lived here; everything was overgrown with new grass.

"Right you lot. Back to help," shouted Dadcu, Mam's father. For what seemed like forever after a long journey, the children helped unpack the boats and tie skins over the holes in the hut thatching. Tomorrow they would need to be thatched with new reeds. Finally they spread out the sleeping furs onto the floor of the huts and collapsed, pretending to snore as if they were totally exhausted. But they soon leapt up again when Mam shouted, "The meat's ready."

Everyone sat round the fire, passing a wooden dish of meat and cooked roots around until they were full. Mam tossed a big bone to each of the dogs, Wuff and Sandy. Sandy sat right behind May Bud and she could hear him crunching.

She leant against her grandmother, Mamgu and listened to the talk.

"How lovely to be at Summer Camp," sighed Mamgu. "No need to move now until the frosts come."

"What a great Meet!" said Rainbow, Mam's sister.

"It was lovely to catch up with all the family and see the new babies," said Mam.

"I enjoyed the dancing most," said Aspen, Mam's other sister. "It's fun with so many people."

"Especially with so many young lads," said Mamgu with a smile. "We noticed you liked dancing with that lad from Long Island. Are we going to see more of him in future?"

"I doubt it," said Aspen. "He was really boring. But he had such a wonderful beaver skin cap."

"That's why Rainbow chose me," said Wild Wave.

"Yes, I loved stroking his beaver skin cap," laughed Rainbow.

"Well, we could do with a new young lad around," said Dad to Aspen. "now that Dadcu is getting so old and past it!"

"You young pighog!" said Dadcu, knocking Dad's cap off his head. "I'm fitter and stronger than you! The cheek!"

When they had stopped laughing Dad said, "It was quite a haul back from Summer Meet with all our stuff in the boats. You're getting heavy now, Wolf. I think we'll make you your own boat while we're here at Summer Camp."

"Ooh," said Wolf. "Am I strong enough to paddle my own boat?"

"We'll make you a half size," said Dad. "Wild Wave and I will go and find a decent lime tree as soon as we get the salmon traps up."

"There was a good one in Sandy Hollow last year," said Dadcu.

"Thanks," said Dad. "We'll head that way and have a look."

It was a beautiful summer evening, warm and moist. May Bud could hear the foxes squealing from inside the wood behind her and, in front of her, the gentle lap, lap of the waves of the River against the shore. A great flock of starlings flew overhead with a murmuring sound, twisting together to land on the reeds. The sun had just gone down and the ragged edges of the clouds were tinged with pink.

"Red sky at night, fisher's delight," said Mamgu. "It'll be fine tomorrow. But I'm turning in before the mist rises." May Bud wanted to stay there all night but Mamgu was right, the mist was rising on the river and those sleeping furs in the hut would be lovely and warm. They had all summer to enjoy at Goldcliff.

CHAPTER 2

Summer Camp

A few days later May Bud and Crane woke up just as the sun came up. Mam, Dad and Wolf were still asleep so they went out of the hut into the early morning. Mist hung in the air in the Estuary so that they could hardly see the other bank. There was dew on the trampled grass around the huts and on the dogs. As the girls came out Wuff and Sandy got up, stretched and wagged their tails and Crane ran and cuddled them. May Bud stirred the embers of the fire with a stick and put on some new sticks from the pile alongside.

"Blow, Crane!" she said and they blew together until the sticks caught and flames were coming up.

"Poo," said Crane. "Quick, then," said May Bud and taking her hand they scurried along the path through the trees to the reed beds, the dogs racing alongside. Crane was only two and had to get to the toilet as fast as possible. The path to the toilet area was overgrown as no one had had time to cut it back since they arrived. On the way back May Bud cut off some of the smaller branches with her axe that hung from her belt; they carried them back to the fire to dry because they never wasted firewood.

Now everyone was up and they had breakfast, some dried venison left over from the spring hunt in the Welsh Hills. Then Dad said, "Time to set up the salmon traps. Come on everybody." The women had been weaving salmon baskets for the last few days, from split willow that they cut from the trees around the camp, and there was a large stack of baskets on the edge of camp. Everyone carried as many as they could down to the foreshore. The mist had lifted and it was going to be a beautiful summer's day. The tide was going out, leaving gooey mud which they would wade through to get to the stream channel where they would set up the baskets. The baskets were long and thin so that salmon could swim into them at high tide but would not be able to turn around and swim out. All through the summer someone would check the baskets at every low tide, night and day, and the salmon they didn't eat now would be smoked to save for the winter.

The men went off to cut long stakes to fasten the baskets to. Mam, Mamgu and Rainbow sat down with Crane and Rainbow's baby, Rose, while Aspen wandered off to dig up roots in the reeds. But Petal and May Bud went down to the mud. It squidged between their toes. May Bud bent down and picked up a handful of mud and suddenly she smeared it onto Petal's cheek.

"Yuk," said Petal and picking up her own handful of mud she chased May Bud round and round in the mud. May Bud ran off laughing and swerved to avoid Petal, and then she skidded sideways and ended up full length face down in the mud. Petal screamed with laughter. Then she skidded and fell over too. They were both completely covered, dripping with the liquid mud. They trudged back to the shore, laughing. Mam could hardly speak she was laughing so much.

"You look like Mud Monsters," she gasped.

Then it was time to go down to the stream channel. Petal and May Bud's hands were so muddy they kept dropping their baskets. Dad and Wild Wave drove the long stakes onto the mud and Mamgu bound the baskets on with string.

"We're almost out of string," she said.

"I'll make some more tomorrow," Dadcu told her.

So the next day May Bud and Wolf went into the forest with Dadcu to help him make string. Dadcu whistled up the dogs to come with them because there would probably be aurochs in the reed swamp. These were huge wild cows, which could be dangerous.

"They'll have their calves with them," explained Dadcu as they went. "The mothers will attack anything that comes near at this time of year, but the dogs will let us know if they're around and we can get out of their way." He was looking around all the time as they walked.

"What we need are lime trees," said Dadcu. "There is a lovely big one near camp but I used that last year. They need a while to recover."

They looked at several lime trees but Dadcu said they were too small. Then they found a very tall straight-trunked tree. With his axe Dadcu made two long grooves in the bark as far up as far as he could reach. He eased the strip of bark off the shiny inner wood, handing it to Wolf. Then he cut another strip for May Bud and a third for himself. They carried them back to camp and then watched while Dadcu stripped the strands from the inside of the woody bark. It pulled off in long strings. Dadcu dug a long hole with his axe in the wet peaty area down near the River, digging down until the hole flooded, and he carefully laid in the stringy pieces.

"We'll leave them in there till full moon," said Dadcu. "Then we can make string."

"Why do they have to stay in there? They'll get all smelly," asked May Bud.

"All the mess will rot off till you just get the white string strands. Right, now we're picking nettles – we can make some string from them. It's not as good as lime string, but Mamgu needs something now. Bring a basket each."

They walked along the edge of the forest until they found a patch of nettles where an old camp had been. Dadcu picked some large dock leaves, made a wodge of them in his hand and, holding the nettle stems with that hand, he cut off the stems, then laid them in the basket.

"Don't touch them," he laughed. When they had two basketfuls they carefully carried them back to camp. Wolf had wandered off, but May Bud wanted to help. She picked some dock leaves and Dadcu showed her how to hold the nettles so that she didn't get stung. She stripped off the leaves, then Dadcu beat the stalks with a stone to get the fibres out. He took some in his left hand and started twisting them together, producing a short piece of string. Then he wound it round the centre of a stout stick. May Bud held it at both ends, leaning away to take the strain. Dadcu walked backwards adding fibres and twisting gently till they had a long length of string. Then they wound it round the stick.

"Here you are," said Dadcu. "Give it to Mamgu." May Bud proudly presented it to Mamgu.

"Did you make that?" asked Mamgu with a twinkle in her eye. "Just what I needed."

CHAPTER 3

The Boat

A few days later Dad decided to start making Wolf's boat. The day before, he, Dadcu and Wild Wave had chopped down a lime tree with a long straight trunk. Now they hauled it on rollers of tree-trunks through the wood to the camp. All the children gathered round to watch. First Dad and Wild Wave stripped off the bark with their axes. Everyone was encouraged to help but only Aspen managed to chip any bark off. May Bud helped her strip the stringy strands off the bark and they carefully laid them in Dadcu's pit with the others to rot.

The boat would need to be ready before they all went to Winter Camp, so that Wolf could practise using it. The men had lifted the log onto the raised stands to bring it up to working height. Dadcu was chopping off the end of the log; it would be a short boat so that it was light enough for Wolf to paddle. Wild Wave had started to cut out the inside of the boat while Dad shaped the outside.

"What do you want me to do, Dad?" asked Wolf.

"You can help me shape when Dadcu has finished chopping. But until then, can you collect up the wood chips into a basket? Mamgu can use them for smoking."

Though they were working away steadily, the log seemed no nearer to looking like a boat. May Bud and Crane got rather bored and wandered down to the shore. Mam and Mamgu had been down to the salmon traps at low tide and were cleaning the fish and taking out the bones. May Bud and Crane carried a basket of bones and guts and threw them onto the mud for the River to take away. Red kites and buzzards were circling overhead and, as they turned away, one kite swooped down with a cry and snatched something up.

Crane stayed on the mud to watch them sweeping down. May Bud sat down with Mam. She was threading the salmon onto string, two on each piece of string, with sticks tied on either side to stop them curling up.

"That's my string!" said May Bud proudly. "I made it with Dadcu!"

Mamgu pointed to the river. "Look at Crane," she whispered. "She's doing a crane bird dance." Crane was staring at the swooping birds and standing first on one leg, then the other. She was very graceful and looked like the cranes dancing.

"We saw some cranes earlier when we went with Aspen to dig up roots in the rush beds," said May Bud.

Next to them was a wooden structure, two upright timbers at each end with a long pole hung between them at about Mam's height. Mam and Mamgu hung the pairs of salmon fillets over the pole. Underneath they had laid a long fire which Mam now lit with her strike-a-light. Once it was going well, May Bud and Mamgu spread reeds over it to make it smoke, then they all sat down in the sunshine. Aspen came along with two laden baskets, one full of roots, the other full of seeds.

"They'll be lovely," said Mamgu. "I look forward to eating them". Aspen sat down beside them.

It was obvious that they were going to stay chatting in the sun and watching the salmon-smoking fire, so May Bud took Crane back to see how the boat was getting on. It was a very slow job. Even with four of them working on the boat, it took several weeks to finish it. They had first to carve out the inside for Wolf to kneel in. Wild Wave sometimes lit a fire inside the boat to char the wood and make it easier to cut out. Dad shaped the outside of the log with Wolf's help. It was pointed at the front to ride over the waves in the River, and flat underneath so that it would not roll over when it was loaded. Wolf would need to be able to paddle it against the tides and currents along the River banks and across the deep water to the other side.

The final stage was to smooth the rough chopped wood both inside and out, and to carve the prow figurehead. Wolf had a red kite's head on the front of his boat.

Finally came the day when the boat was finished. Everyone gathered on the shore and watched Wolf push his boat into the water. Mam and Mamgu were both crying.

"My baby has his own boat," sniffed Mam. Wolf clambered in and dipped his paddle into the water. The boat shot forward and wobbled from side to side but Wolf kept his balance and shot off into the current. Everyone cheered.

CHAPTER 4

Up the river with Mamgu

One day Mamgu asked May Bud to help her go upriver to look at the eel traps. She had asked Wolf but he was helping Dad mend the spears in time for the boar hunt. While Mamgu was getting the baskets May Bud watched Dad carefully shaping a wooden shaft with his flint knife to get it absolutely straight. Wolf was cutting a groove in the top of another shaft. He then dipped a stick into the blob of wood glue warming on a stone by the fire. He smeared a blob of glue along the groove and Dad carefully stuck in the small flint blades. Dad put down the spear for the glue to set while they made the grooves on the next shaft.

"I'm ready," called Mamgu and she and May Bud went down to the edge of the saltmarsh to her boat.

They had to push the boat over the mud down to the River as the tide was going out. May Bud was glad to feel her hot feet sinking through the cool mud, though it was hard work to wade through the nearer they got to the water. They had to push the boat around huge tree trunks. There was a lovely smell of seaweed and a light breeze. Above, a peregrine called. When they got to the river, the herons standing in the shallow water fishing for little crabs turned to look at them and the nearer ones took off.

May Bud tried to talk on the way up the River, but Mamgu was short of breath paddling against the current and couldn't reply. The eel traps were in shallow water at the edge of the river, next to a patch of reeds and rushes. Willows grew in the shallows and May Bud could hear the wind rustling in the leaves of the trees, as if they were

whispering. There were lots of eels in the traps, some very large who fought to get away. They were very slippery, but Mamgu managed to catch most of them and put them in her basket.

The way back was much easier. Mamgu could let the current take the boat, just pointing it in the right direction with her paddle. So May Bud could ask her questions.

"Mamgu, what was it like when you were a little girl?"

"It was the same as today. Except the hazelnut trees didn't have nearly so many nuts. My Mamgu trimmed them with her axe one autumn, close to the ground. We stacked the logs to dry for next year. I thought she'd killed them. I cried and cried. But next spring when we came back they were sprouting again and look at them now, covered in nuts. It will soon be time to cut them again."

"Did you have hazelnuts that next year?"

Mamgu paddled hard on the right side of the boat to turn it out of the main current and towards the bank. "Well no, not for a few years. But there was a good bush up on Speckedly Point so we didn't go without. That fell into the sea the year I had your mam."

"So has the Valley been just like this since the Great Bear made the world?"

"Oh no," said Mamgu. "My Dadcu used to tell a story that his Dadcu told him. When he was a little boy, there was just a river running down the middle of the valley. You had to go a day's journey downstream to see the sea. There were salmon and eels but no seals and the River didn't taste salty. There were trees right down to the River, so they used to camp down on the bank. Then there was a big storm and the River rose and rose until it covered the camp and the Forest. They all got in their boats and it was a terrible struggle to get upstream because of the surge of water, swirling and trying to drown them. Dadcu said it was the Wild White Whale trying to eat them all up. Lots of the clan died and the ones that didn't had nothing – no huts, no food, no tools. They had to start again."

"And what happened when the River went down?" asked May Bud.

"It never did go down," said Mamgu as she turned up towards the camp. "We still have it now. Those great trees in the mud at low tide – those are the trees of the Forest that was flooded. They all died. They stood for years like great stalks in the saltmarsh until they fell into the

water." May Bud looked back at her beloved River with new eyes. It filled the width of the valley, a huge rolling grey mass, full of fish and crabs.

Mamgu paddled to the beach, then got out into the water and pushed the boat up onto the shore. Before they got out she looked carefully to make sure there were no aurochs in the reed beds.

"Your dad saw some here yesterday, " she said to May Bud, "but they must have moved on."

May Bud helped to lug the baskets of eels onto land. Then they sat on the bank threading the eels onto string.

"Keep them even, May Bud," said Mamgu. "We want a bit of a gap in between." They tied the strings onto the eel racks and Mamgu lit a fire underneath.

"Get some damp reeds on that fire," said Mamgu. "We need plenty of smoke."

So May Bud got out her flint knife from her pouch and walked to and fro cutting reeds and throwing them onto the fire. Whenever she saw a flame Mamgu would shout and May Bud ran to put some more on top. Finally it grew dark and Mamgu said they would leave the fire to smoulder. Later they would take the eels off and pack them in baskets.

May Bud still had some questions. "Mamgu, will Wolf have to go away when he grows up."

"Why do you ask, child?"

"Well, Mam's sisters live with us but her brothers we only see at Summer Camp."

"Well, Wolf will want to explore and see the world when he gets older – it's what boys do. You can go away if you want to but most girls stay with their Mams. One day you'll be a mam and she'll help you with the birth and bringing up. Then you'll be going out getting food for your children and it helps if you know where the blackberries are."

"In the nook," said May Bush immediately.

"And the raspberries? "

"On the edge of the oak wood."

"And the best crab apples," asked Mamgu with a little smile.

"Err... down at the back of Goldcliff."

"And where would you go if you wanted a new axe handle?"

"I'd wait till I got to winter camp. The red deer often drop their antlers up by the alder wood on the side of the Wye," said May Bud.

"You see," said Mamgu, "If you moved away you'd have to learn all this again in a new place. Hunting is the same everywhere. Wolf will find a girl at Summer Camp and live with her family. Her father and brothers will point him in the right direction." May Bud giggled at the thought of her scrawny brother finding a girl.

"He could get one across the River," she said.

"You have to be careful you're not related," said Mamgu severely. "I knew a girl who had a baby with her brother. It died at birth."

"Oh," said May Bud and was glad to run over and play with Crane.

Next day she and Mamgu went to take down the smoked eels and pack them away in baskets for the winter, but May Bud didn't ask Mamgu any more questions!

CHAPTER 5

Wolf's boat

olf went out every day in his boat, usually with Dad or Dadcu alongside. He could turn using his paddle and after several days he could almost keep up with Dad - though not with Dadcu, who, as he had said, was stronger and fitter than Dad. Wolf overturned several times but managed to right the boat on his own. One day Dad allowed him to take Sandy and Wuff with him. When they got back safely, despite the dogs walking about in the boat causing it to wobble, Dad said Wolf could go out on his own.

"But only along the bank near the reeds," warned Dad. "You're not good enough to go into the River currents yet."

Wolf raced up into camp and grabbed May Bud's arm. "I can go out in my boat on my own now," he shouted.

"Ooh, can I come with you," said May Bud. "Can Petal come too? Pleeease!"

"Yes, course," said Wolf. "Do you want to come now? Bring your paddles!"

They raced down to the water's edge. It started to rain as they reached the River. Wolf pushed his boat off and they waded out and climbed in. As it was his boat Wolf sat in the prow, with May Bud in the stern and Petal in between them. They all paddled together. The boat sat heavily in the water with the three of them in it. It lifted as it rose over the waves. Wolf had intended to go upstream hugging the shore, but because they were all paddling on one side of the boat, they gradually turned to the right, facing the opposite bank of the River.

"Where are we going, Wolf?" asked May Bud.

"Just upstream to Reed Bank," he said.

The waves started to get higher and the boat lifted at the front to rise over them. "Aren't we going out a bit far?" asked May Bud nervously.

"I think we need to paddle on the other side." Wolf dipped his paddle sharply on the other side and the front of the boat turned sharply towards the shore. A wave slapped the side of the boat and covered Petal with salt water. She squealed and dropped her paddle, fortunately inside the boat. The boat rocked and Petal clung to each side, whimpering. She shivered in the rain.

"Paddle, Wolf!" said May Bud fiercely. They worked as fast as they could but the boat had been taken by the current and slowly drifted out sideways into the main channel. The waves rose so that they could hardly see the shore on either side. They paddled and paddled but could make no headway. Wolf could see that one of the sandbanks in the centre of the River was exposed.

"We'll make for that, he panted. "I think the tide's going out, so we can rest there and come back when the tide goes down."

"You think the tide's going out!" thought May Bud, but she didn't say anything. She had no breath left for speaking anyway.

"Help us, Petal," shouted Wolf. "You won't feel so cold if you paddle." Petal dipped her paddle into the water, but she was only four and had little strength to paddle against the main current of the River.

Unfortunately as they reached the sandbank and landed the waves seemed to be covering it.

"The tide's not going out, it's coming in!" shouted May Bud. "We're going to drown! We can't paddle back. I haven't got any more strength." She screamed. "We're going to die!" Petal was screaming too, holding onto the sides of the boat.

"No, we're not," shouted Wolf. "Look, we're much nearer the other bank. We can paddle over and land there." In despair May Bud looked at the brown water sweeping past and the steep cliffs in front of them.

"We'll just get swept away," she moaned. "There's nowhere to land anyway even if we could get over there." The waves nudged the boat and May Bud and Petal screamed again. Then suddenly the waves swept the boat off the sand bank.

"Paddle!" shouted Wolf and all three plunged their paddles into the water at the same time. With a great burst of energy, and paddling in time with one another, they swept towards the cliffs. Wolf steered by paddling on the other side from the girls and they landed on a tiny rocky beach under the cliffs. Wolf leapt out and pulled the boat clear of the waves. Shakily May Bud and Petal climbed out and they all huddled together.

"Can we climb up?" asked Petal.

"I don't think so," said Wolf, looking up doubtfully. "It's too high. But when the tide goes down we can get back across the river," he said with confidence which he did not really feel. They sat down to wait in the shelter at the base of the cliff. All of them were hungry but nobody mentioned it because they had nothing to eat.

Then May Bud realised that she had her strike-a-light in her pouch and she collected some driftwood.

"Pick some dry grass, you two," she said.

"Easier said than done in this rain," grumbled Wolf, but they managed to get some dead flower heads. With Petal and Wolf leaning over her to shelter her from the rain May Bud managed to get a flame out of the dried flowers and piled the driftwood on top. The fire was very smoky but gave out lots of warmth and they started to dry off. This cheered them all up considerably, even more so when Wolf found some dried seal meat in his pouch.

They had just started singing when, joy of joys! a boat appeared round the cliff and landed on to their little beach. They were saved! In the boat was a man they had never seen before.

"You OK?" he asked. "I was up on the top and saw you heading for the cliff. My name's Beaver by the way."

May Bud and Petal looked at Wolf to explain. "We're from the other side, from Goldcliff," he said. "We got swept away by the current. It's my first boat. I was only supposed to go along the bank," he admitted looking down at his feet.

"Well, we'd better get you home, though you're quite cosy here. Who lit the fire?"

"I did," said May Bud shyly.

"Well done," he said. May Bud felt very clever and less shy. "Is that a beaver skin hat?" she asked.

"Yes," said Beaver, taking it off to show her. May Bud and Petal stroked it.

"We caught it up the Avon river. Who wants some salmon?" They chewed the delicious smoked salmon while Beaver got out a spare cloak for Wolf who was shivering.

Then Beaver tied Wolf's boat to the back of his own and collected their paddles. He loaded them all in and gave instructions about which side they were to paddle. Then he pushed off. The current immediately whipped the boat downstream but with Beaver's strong paddling he managed to start crossing the River.

Finally they arrived back at Goldcliff. They were met by a party of boats and a group of frantic relatives on the shore. Dad had noticed that Wolf's boat had disappeared and had been searching for them; everyone had feared the worst. After the children had been scolded, Beaver was invited into camp for a large meal. As they walked up May Bud pulled Aspen back. "He's got a Beaver skin cap," she said.

Aspen and Beaver got on very well and Beaver often visited the camp during the summer. One evening Dadcu asked Beaver to list his ancestors. Beaver stood up. "I am Beaver son of Red Oak son of Fast Burn son of White Eagle...." It went on for a long time. Then he listed his mother's family.

"Why are they doing this?" Wolf asked his father.

"To make sure that Beaver and Aspen aren't related, in case they have children," said Dad. Wolf and May Bud looked at one another. Perhaps Beaver would be coming to live with them.

CHAPTER 6

Boar hunt

May Bud was helping to collect firewood to stack for next year. "Why do we have to collect it now?" she moaned.

"So that it's seasoned and ready to light the fire when we get back next year," said Mam carrying her armful of wood on the route back to the campsite. "We'll be going soon to Winter Camp and we want everything ready for when we leave."

"I know that," said May Bud. "But why do I have to do it? It's not fair... Wolf gets out of all the boring jobs. He's on the boar hunt today. He gets all the fun. Why can't I go on boar hunts?"

"You know you're too young." May Bud stuck out her lower lip and set down her measly small pile of sticks. She folded her arms as if to say, "I'm not doing any more."

"I won't be able to go even when I'm old like you."

Mam stopped and looked at her, then she sighed, put down her logs and gave May Bud a long hug. Crane cuddled up and hugged May Bud from the back. "I felt like you when I was young. But now I realise that girls are too important to go hunting. Can Dad have babies?"

"No, of course not," said May Bud, snorting at the thought of Dad pregnant.

"Well then," said Mam solemnly. "Hunting is dangerous. Our tasks may be less exciting but they are essential. Most of our food comes from the fish we catch and the plants we gather. Next year we'll all be glad of the wood you've collected." May Bud slowly picked up her sticks and they moved on.

They heard a crashing to their right and Aspen appeared pulling a rough sledge piled with logs. "Here's Aspen with a good load," shouted May Bud.

"Asthpen," lisped Crane.

"I can't wait for the boar hunt to finish," said Aspen. "This will be the first time Beaver will be eating with us as part of the family now he's been hunting. He says he'll come to Winter Camp with us." She picked up Crane and swung her round. "Yummy boar, yummy boar!" she shouted and Mam started singing to encourage them all back to the camp. [The song is sung to the tune of *The animals went in two by two, Hurrah! Hurrah!*]

The boar went goring to and fro, Hurrah! Hurrah!
The boar went goring to and fro, Hurrah! Hurrah!
The boar went goring to and fro,
And everyone hid to see him go,
And the boar went home with apples on his tusks.

Crane swung her head to left and right in time to the music as she stomped along. They all joined in singing loudly:

The boar went trampling past the bay, Hurrah! Hurrah!
The boar went trampling past the bay, Hurrah! Hurrah!
The boar went trampling past the bay,
The stripey piglets ran away,
And the boar went home with apples on his tusks.

The boar gored slowly right and left, Hurrah! Hurrah!
The boar gored slowly right and left, Hurrah! Hurrah!
The boar gored slowly right and left,
The spearsman got him in the chest,
And the boar went home with apples on his tusks.

Mam cooked him fast and cooked him slow, Hurrah! Hurrah!
Mam cooked him fast and cooked him slow, Hurrah! Hurrah!
Mam cooked him fast and cooked him slow,
We ate him up to make us grow!
And the boar went home with apples on his tusks.

They arrived back and stacked the logs at the side of the camp. "What's goring, Mam?" asked May Bud. "In the song, the boar went goring."

Mam tucked her legs under her and took Crane on her lap for a feed. "You know the tusks the boar has? Dadcu has some huge boar tusks in his ceremonial necklace that he wears for the summer dancing." May Bud nodded. "Well, the boar tosses his head from side to side and gores you with his tusks if you get in his way. It's very dangerous if he gores you."

"Will Wolf get gored?" asked May Bud anxiously.

"You know how fast Wolf can move. He'll skip out of the way. But you remember Great Dadcu, Dadcu's father?" May Bud nodded. "Remember the great scar he had on his arm."

"Was that done by a boar?" May Bud remembered that scar. His arm was bumpy and mauve from hand to elbow.

Mam nodded. "They had to fetch Great Mamgu from upriver at Craneswater to look after him. She was a wonderful shaman. She fetched the Crane spirit from the other world to help heal it. She put in some puffball and sewed up the gored gash."

"Sewed it up. Ugh! What with?"

"I think she used otter gut. The best is cat gut but they are so difficult to catch."

"You mean like you sew clothes?" May Bud fingered the join in her skirt, ridged with neat stitching.

"Yes." Mam put Crane down and gave her some dried eel to chew on. She looked round at the preparations and started to lay the fire in the firepit, ready for the cooking.

"But doesn't it hurt?"

"Of course it hurts! But Great Dadcu was a mighty warrior so he could stand it. And Great Mamgu gave him some firewater to drink." That reminded May Bud and she stirred the firewater in its wooden trough. She didn't really like firewater. It burnt the back of your throat when you drank it and made you cough. But the grownups had it for special occasions. She noticed it made Mam giggle and Dad got very loud.

"I would like to be a healer when I grow up," said May Bud solemnly. "It would be wonderful to go to the spirit world and heal people."

Mamgu and Rainbow were coming up from the shore carrying between them a basket of roots, Rose swaying about and shouting in the basket on Rainbow's back. Petal had another basket with large wet leaves in.

"Ooh, look," said Mam. "They've done well. I'll get them roots steaming on the hot rocks in the fire pit."

Just then they heard crashing in the reeds and shouting.

"They're here," shouted Mam and they all ran towards the noise. Wolf was first out of the trees. Mam caught him in her arms and hugged him.

"Let me down," struggled Wolf. "I'm a warrior now." He showed May Bud and Crane the blood on his forehead. "They blooded me with the tongue," he said proudly. "I get to eat the liver."

Then the men came through the trees. Beaver and Wild Wave carried the spears. A huge dead boar with its feet tied together was swinging from a long stick carried by Dad and Dadcu. They threw the boar down next to the fire.

"That was heavy," grunted Dadcu. "Particularly carrying it over the saltmarsh."

"But wonderful eating," said Mamgu. "Now you men relax. We've got firewater for you to drink and a trough to pick at while we get this cooking."

The girls cut up the boar once Mamgu had skinned it, while Mam got the fire in the pit red hot. Then Rainbow helped Petal wrap the pieces of meat in the large wet leaves that she had picked and Mam and Mamgu laid them on top of the hot rocks and charcoal and covered everything with soil.

"There," said Mam. Now they could drink firewater and tell stories till it was ready.

CHAPTER 7

The Feast

Before the family could eat the boar, Mamgu had to send the spirit of the boar to the Island of the Spirits. Everyone quietly watched as Wild Wave helped her to lift the boar's head onto the tall stake on the edge of Camp. She stuffed some apples into his mouth, then pushed two apples onto his tusks.

"That's why he has apples on his tusks in the song," whispered May Bud to Mam.

"That's right," Mam whispered back. Mamgu and Wild Wave lifted the heavy skin of the boar and draped it over the stake. His legs hung down on either side. Then slowly and quietly Mamgu sang the last verse of the song:

> *The boar went galloping to the Isle, Hurrah! Hurrah!*
> *The boar went galloping to the Isle, Hurrah! Hurrah!*
> *The boar went galloping to the Isle,*
> *And all the ancestors had to smile*
> *As the boar came home with apples on his tusks!*

"Listen," she said," and you'll hear him galloping home." May Bud listened in the evening quiet and far away she could hear the galloping of hooves.

"All right," said Mamgu, "he's gone. Now everyone," and they all sang as loudly as they could:

The boar went galloping to the Isle, Hurrah! Hurrah!
The boar went galloping to the Isle, Hurrah! Hurrah!
The boar went galloping to the Isle,
And all the ancestors had to smile
As the boar came home with apples on his tusks!

"So, how was the hunt then?" asked Mamgu as she settled round the fire. Everyone looked at Dadcu.

"He wasn't the largest boar we saw," he said. "There was a much larger one but he got away."

"Perhaps he was the Great Boar," suggested Aspen.

"He might have been," said Dadcu. "But this one was big enough, so we followed him. He led us a merry dance but the dogs cornered him up by Grey Hill and we speared him."

"You had to carry him all the way back from there?" asked Mam.

"We took it in turns," said Dad. He looked with pride at Wolf. "Wolf got a spear stroke in. We've got a mighty warrior there in the making." Then everyone looked at Wolf, who seemed as though he would burst with pride.

"Well done, Wolf," said Mamgu. "You'll be able to have the tusks as a necklace for The Meet dances. Now, Dadcu, tell us the story of the Great Boar."

"You've heard it so many times," objected Dadcu.

"The little ones haven't."

"And it's such a good tale," pleaded Aspen.

"Well. Once upon a time, a long while ago, in the time of the making of the world, when the Great White Whale walked on the River and the First People lived in the Valley, there was a man called Raven."

"Why was he called Raven?" asked Wolf. Normally Dadcu was annoyed at being interrupted but Wolf was allowed today as this was his First Hunt Feast.

"Why are you called Wolf?"

"Because the wolves were howling when I was born."

"They were looking for food in the snow," said Mam. "And freezing it was too on the day of your birth." Everyone laughed.

Aspen was passing around the wooden trough loaded with cooked roots, berries and venison strips. She offered it to Wild Wave. "Why were you called Wild Wave," she asked.

"Umm," he said. "These roots are delicious. Well, just as I was born the wave passed along the River and it was the largest any one had seen."

"We called May Bud that because the May flowers came out the day after she was born," said Mam. "And Crane because the cranes were dancing when she was born and she had such long gangly legs."

"The petals of the apple tree fell on me as Petal was born..." started Rainbow.

"Anyway..." broke in Dadcu and they all laughed and settled down for the story.

"Perhaps a raven croaked when he was born. But Raven was well named. He was so black-hearted he'd eat the dead. Well, one day he killed a man, the elder of his clan, not by mistake, but deliberately. All the other men got together and trailed him, with the dogs sniffing him out. They trailed him for three days, but he was a mighty hunter and knew how to get away. But they got closer all the time. And finally his only way to go was up a mountain. He got to the top and he could see the dogs and men coming out of the trees. So he shouted out to the Raven Spirit, "Save me." And the Raven Spirit (who was as black-hearted as he was) liked Raven for killing the man, for Raven Spirit would be able to gorge upon the corpse. So in return he turned Raven into a boar, a huge boar with huge tusks and bristles so sharp and stiff you could stand an apple up on them. He was so fierce the men chased and fought with him but he always got away. And he's still roaming the woods of the River, but he can never be caught."

They listened spell bound to Dadcu's stories until finally Mamgu said, "I'll have a look at the meat," and she found it was ready. Aspen and Mam handed around the troughs piled high with delicious boar meat until everyone was stuffed and one by one fell asleep around the fire. Before she fell asleep May Bud looked up at the boar on the edge of the Camp.

"Thank you," she whispered. "Enjoy your apples."

CHAPTER 8

Autumn harvest

After the feast there was enough boar meat left to smoke for the winter. Wolf and May Bud helped Mam cut it into long strips and hang it over the fire.

"It needs longer than the salmon and the eels," said Mamgu. "We need to get all the smoking finished because we will have to go to Winter Camp soon. See how the leaves are starting to turn colour."

The next few days were full of jobs. Most days the women and girls were out fruit-picking: first the raspberries on the woodland edge, then there was so much to pick they were out from first light to dusk: blackberries, elderberries and crab apples, sloes and wild plums. Mamgu looked after Crane and Rose and they helped her to dry the fruit and pack it in the baskets. May Bud could remember being left in the camp and was proud to be part of the picking party this year, even if her hands were stained, and aching with nettle stings and blackberry prickles. How good that salmon cooked with berries tasted when they got back!

The men were hunting deer in the woods; when they caught one everyone had to help skin it and hang the meat to smoke. May Bud and Petal kept an eye on the fire and cut reeds to make it smoky. They had to go down to the foreshore, though the nearest reeds were in the toilet area, but they couldn't use reeds from there! Rainbow and Aspen stretched the deer skins with the fur still attached onto wooden frames so that they would dry hard and flat. When they got to winter camp everyone would help to rub in animal fat to make the skins supple again.

"They'll make lovely clothes when the bad weather comes," said Mamgu, stroking the fur. "You need some new shoes, Wolf."

"I like bare feet," said Wolf scornfully. "Hunters need to creep quietly through the wood, not scuffle in shoes."

"You'll be glad of shoes in the snow!" laughed Mam, but Wolf stalked off to join his dad.

"He's growing up," said Mam sadly.

When they weren't hunting the men went out burning. They set fire to the reedswamp so that next year the lush new shoots would make good grazing and attract animals, which would be easier to hunt. Clouds of smoke drifted across the River.

The men came rushing into camp covered in black soot, frightening the youngsters and pretending to get soot all over Mamgu, Mam and Rainbow.

"Get off!" laughed Mam as Dad took her face in his sooty hands. "You stink! And you're frightening Crane." Crane didn't realise it was her father in the disguise and his face did look weird with the whites of his eyes shining out of the darkness.

Then came the rains. It was raining when they woke up and all day long. Everything was wet. May Bud shivered in her skirt until Mam made her put on her fur cape and otter skin hat. They had been made last year and the cape was too small and the cap only just fitted. Mam looked at her smiling.

"When we get to winter camp you'll be the first one to get new clothes," she promised.

With the damp came the mushrooms and fungi. Some of the fungi had to be eaten immediately, so one night Mamgu cooked venison stuffed with mushrooms. It was delicious. The rest of the fungi she threaded on strings to dry over the fires. By now she had fires going all round the camp.

Finally it was time for the hazelnuts and then came the first frost: the grass was white when they woke up and they left footprints on the way to the toilet area.

"My feet are cold," moaned Wolf as he hopped back into camp. Mam said nothing but brought out his last years' shoes and helped him loosen the ties so they would fit. Then she gave him a hug and kissed the top of his head. To her surprise he hugged her back.

That night Mamgu told everyone that they would be moving to Winter Camp at the next highest tide which would be at full moon. Dad looked at the moon. "Day after tomorrow then," he said, "We'd better start packing first light."

So first thing in the morning everyone was up. Everything in camp had to be carried down to the shore. Dad and Wild Wave pulled the boats up above the beach. There were eight boats now that Wolf had his own and Beaver was joining them, but there was a great deal to put in. There were baskets and more baskets and wooden boxes, all full of food. There were weapons, bows and arrows, bundles of string, baskets of cooking stones, and boxes of clothes. All the women each had a small box of equipment and Mamgu had a box of dried plants in case of illness or injury.

The last thing to pack was the huts. Everyone helped to carry the sleeping furs down to the boats. The wooden frames would stay here until next summer. May Bud hated it when everything had been taken away. It looked as though the camp had died, with just the huts left standing. Around the fire were thrown away bones, gnawed by the dogs, and other rubbish: old tools, broken baskets, fragments of wooden boxes.

"Never mind, May Bud," said Mam giving her a hug. "We'll be back next summer to enjoy it all again." She banked up the fire; in the morning she would take some of the hot embers, wrap them in green leaves and put them in a birch bark tub so that when they arrived at Winter Camp she could start a fire immediately in Winter House. That night they slept in the boats. May Bud and Crane were wedged between a basket of salmon and a wooden box of clothes. Fortunately it was dry, but it was very cold.

Just as the sun came up everyone was awake and eating some dried eel and salmon. Mam brought the fire box down from camp. She had poured water on the fire so that it had gone out for the first time since they had arrived from The Meet. The tide was coming in with a hissing sound.

"We're off!" said Dadcu. One by one he pushed the boats off from the shore and their owners waded out and climbed in. Wild Wave went first and Dad handed Petal into his boat. Then he got in and Dadcu lifted May Bud in next to him. Mamgu followed, then came Aspen with the dogs and Beaver in his boat. Wolf jumped into his little boat and paddled over to be next to Dad. Crane and Mam came next, and Rainbow in her boat with baby Rose. Dadcu was the last to leave. Everyone waited until he had safely climbed into his boat, then as a group they all dipped their paddles into the water and slowly headed up river on the long way to Winter Camp.

WHAT WE KNOW ABOUT LIFE AT GOLDCLIFF 7500 YEARS AGO FROM ARCHAEOLOGY AND THE LIVES OF MODERN HUNTER-GATHERERS

As much as possible this book is based on archaeology. I have been helping my husband Martin Bell dig at Goldcliff in South Wales for years. We have found the place where May Bud and her family came for Summer Camp. We have dug up their house sites, their fires and their food waste. We have found their stone and flint tools, and their footprints in the mud of the river.

There were no towns and no villages. We think that at Goldcliff they lived for part of the summer and the autumn in small round huts, probably thatched with reeds. The food they ate came from the wild: meat from hunting animals, fish from the Estuary, and vegetables and fruit from wild plants. They had no domestic animals except dogs.

We know that people came back to the same campsite regularly for at least 1000 years – that is as long ago for us as the Battle of Hastings.

There are lots of things we can't know from archaeology about life in those days: their songs, how they did their hair, what their clothes looked like. However, we can look at people who still live as hunter-gatherers today, in different parts of the world, to help us to reconstruct their life. These are the ancestors of modern Welsh people, but we don't know what language they spoke. I have given them names based on natural things in the world around them.

Chapter 1: From Summer Meet to Summer Camp

Journey to Summer Camp: most modern hunter-gatherers move several times each year because each area would have different types of food (plants and animals) and materials for tools. Our digs show that they came to Goldcliff in summer to autumn. At The Meet lots of groups would get together and exchange things that they could not get in their own areas.

Beaver cap: clothes were made of furs and skins. Beavers used to live in Britain, and their bones and gnawed wood have been found on prehistoric sites in the Severn Estuary, though not at Goldcliff. Beavers have recently been reintroduced to Britain.

Chapter 2: Summer Camp

Toilet: we found worm cysts in the soil next to the place where people camped, so this was the toilet area. Before modern times most people had worms in their guts which would come out in their poo.

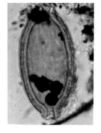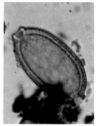

Fishing: we have found parts of wooden fish traps at Goldcliff, and fish baskets are known from sites in Ireland and Europe. We also have some salmon bones and lots of eel bones.

Aurochs: these were wild cattle. They were much larger than modern cows. We know from bone finds that people at Goldcliff hunted and ate them. In Newport Museum you can see an aurochs skeleton.

Footprints: we have footprints in the mud at Goldcliff of men, women and children. In one area two children aged 5 and 11 were chasing about and having fun as May Bud and Petal did. Footprints of people and deer have also been found at Uskmouth.

String: people did make string from tree and nettle fibres. We have bits of string from archaeological sites, though not from Goldcliff.

Chapter 3: The Boat

Boat: we have no boats from Goldcliff, but boats carved from single logs (called dug-outs) and wooden paddles have been found in Denmark, Holland and Ireland. The boats were often made from lime trees.

Cranes: we have lots of bird footprints in the mud at Goldcliff, including cranes, herons, oyster catchers and dunlins. Cranes were common when May Bud was alive. They have recently been reintroduced and are nesting in the Somerset Levels and at the Newport Wetlands.

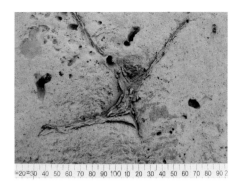

Smoked salmon: modern hunter-gatherers smoke fish and meat to preserve it for the winter when there is less fresh food to catch.

Chapter 4: Up the river with Mamgu

Small flint blades: tiny tools called microliths were fitted into wooden shafts and handles to make arrows, knives and other tools.

The submerged forest: this still survives on the foreshore. There are submerged forests all around the coasts of Britain. The sea level rose suddenly years before May Bud was a girl and flooded the forest, so in her day great tall dead trees stood in the mud. The sea has since risen even more and flooded the site where May Bud lived.

Peregrines and herons: these still live in the Severn Estuary valley today.

Hazelnuts, raspberries etc: we have found all these nuts and fruits from sieving soil samples from our excavations.

Axe: Four of these stone axes were found at Goldcliff.

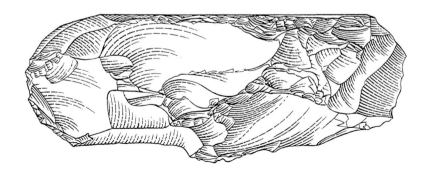

Red deer antler handle for axe: this axe handle from Goldcliff (now in the National Museum in Cardiff) once had a stone axe set in it, but the handle broke and was thrown away.

Chapter 5: Wolf's boat

Lighting the fire: Everyone would be able to light a fire in May Bud's time.

Seal meat: we have seal bones at Goldcliff.

Chapter 6: Boar hunt

Boar bones: we have found cooked wild boar bones at Goldcliff so we know they ate boar.

Hot stones: we have lots of cracked stones that were heated and then had water put on them, to make steam and cook food.

Chapter 7: The Feast

We don't know anything about beliefs at this time, so this chapter is based on modern hunter-gatherers. The story of the boar is similar to an old Welsh story in the Mabinogion about a man turned into a boar, who could never be caught.

Wolves: we have a pawprint from a wolf or dog, and animal bones chewed by wolves, dogs or foxes.

Boar tusk: we found a boar tusk at Goldcliff.

The Wave: a tidal wave travels up the River Estuary with spring tides twice a month. Today this is called the Severn Bore.

Chapter 8: Autumn Harvest

Burning: we know that the people of Goldcliff (and all over Britain) burnt vegetation to clear areas, to produce more grazing for animals and help food plants to grow.

Red deer: we have bones of roe deer and red deer and there are red deer footprints at Goldcliff and Uskmouth.

Otter skin hat: we have otter bones from Goldcliff and cut marks on them show that the otters were skinned.

Berries: all these fruits have been found in soil samples at Goldcliff: crab apple, sloe, raspberry and elderberry. They probably also ate other fruits like blackberries and wild plums.

Mushrooms: we assume people ate mushrooms.

Fire: the fire in a birch bark basket is based on a later example. A man preserved in ice in the Alps in Italy (the Ice Man) had embers in a birch bark basket. He died about 5200 years ago.

Dawn, Goldcliff (Chris Harris / Living Levels)

You can visit the Gwent Levels in South Wales where May Bud and her family lived and see the Severn Estuary, the reed beds and the saltmarsh. The cranes are nesting again and the starlings still murmur in clouds as they come to roost at dusk. Otters still live on the Levels, and wild boars and beavers can now be found nearby in the Forest of Dean, but aurochs died out about 3400 years ago and wolves about 200 years ago.

It is not possible to visit any of the archaeological sites without a guide. The foreshore is a dangerous place, with quicksand, deep mud and slippery rocks over which the tide comes in rapidly, and the archaeological sites are fragile and easily damaged. The site is also a Nature Reserve and a sensitive habitat for birds. Visitors are encouraged to look from the seawall and imagine what the landscape was like rather than venturing on to the foreshore.

For more information about the Gwent Levels visit:

www.livinglevels.org.uk